D1123197

Skyscrapers and Towers

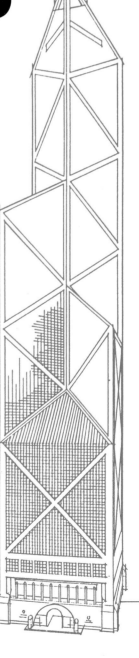

Chris Oxlade

RSVP

RAINTREE
STECK-VAUGHN
P U B L I S H E R S
The Steck-Vaughn Company

Austin, Texas

Published by Raintree Steck-Vaughn Publishers, an imprint of Steck-Vaughn Company

Library of Congress Cataloging-in-Publication Data

Oxlade, Chris.
    Skyscrapers and towers / Chris Oxlade.
      p.   cm. — (Superstructures)
    Includes index.
    Summary: Describes how skyscrapers are different from towers and how both are constructed.
    ISBN 0-8172-4329-1
    1. Skyscrapers — Design and construction — Juvenile literature.   2. Towers — Design and construction — Juvenile literature.   [1. Skyscrapers — Design and construction.   2. Towers — Design and construction.]   I. Title.   II. Series.
TH1615.095   1997
690 — dc20   96-5166
                                                      CIP   AC

Printed in Spain
Bound in the United States
1 2 3 4 5 6 7 8 9 0 LB 99 98 97 96

Designer: Hayley Cove
Editors: Christine Hatt, Pam Wells
Illustrator: John York
Picture research: Juliet Duff
Consultant: Stephen Furnell

Photographic credits
Arcaid: p. 9 top right Denis Gilbert, p. 15 right Ian Lambot,
pp. 15, 32 center Richard Bryant.
Otis plc: p. 35.
Ove Arup and Partners: pp. 17 center right, 18, 19, 31.
© Superstock: cover
Zefa Picture Library: p. 15 left.

The publisher would also like to thank the following for providing references:
Firetex – Leigh's Paints for the furnace test illustrations on page 20;
Takenaka Corporation, Japan for the Sky City 1000 illustrations on page 37.
The architects of the Millennium Tower on page 36 are Sir Norman Foster and Partners.

Note to the reader:
Words in **bold** appear in the glossary on page 46.

Contents

Skyscrapers

Skyscrapers are among the most impressive human-made structures in the world. If you stand at the bottom of one and look up, its sides seem never-ending as they reach hundreds of feet into the sky. Inside a skyscraper, the floors are light and feel lofty. From the highest windows you can see far into the distance.

What's inside?

From the outside, a skyscraper looks simple. But building one is a great feat of organization and engineering skill. The outer wall, called the **cladding**, and the internal finishes hide a complex supporting frame. They also hide hundreds of miles of pipes and cables taking **services,** such as water and electricity, to every story.

Past, present, and future

The first skyscraper was built in Chicago, in 1885. Skyscraper-building spread rapidly, especially in Chicago and New York. These cities now hold most of the world's great skyscrapers, including the Empire State Building and the World Trade Center in New York, and the John Hancock Center and Sears Tower in Chicago. The Sears Tower is the tallest skyscraper in the world now. But the twin towers in Kuala Lumpur will be 1,462 feet (446m) when completed. There are already plans for buildings 3,280 feet (1,000m) high.

The John Hancock Center in Chicago contains offices and apartments, a restaurant, and a shopping and recreation center on the 44th story.

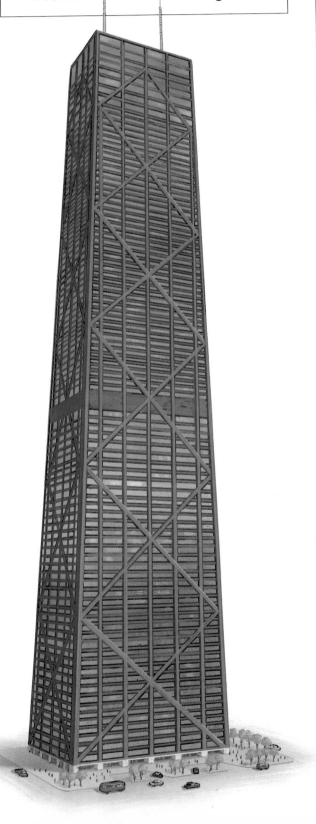

▼ **John Hancock Center Factfile**

Height:	1,128 feet (344m)
Stories:	100
Capacity:	2,000 residents and 5,000 office workers
Completed:	1969
Architects:	Skidmore Owings Merrill

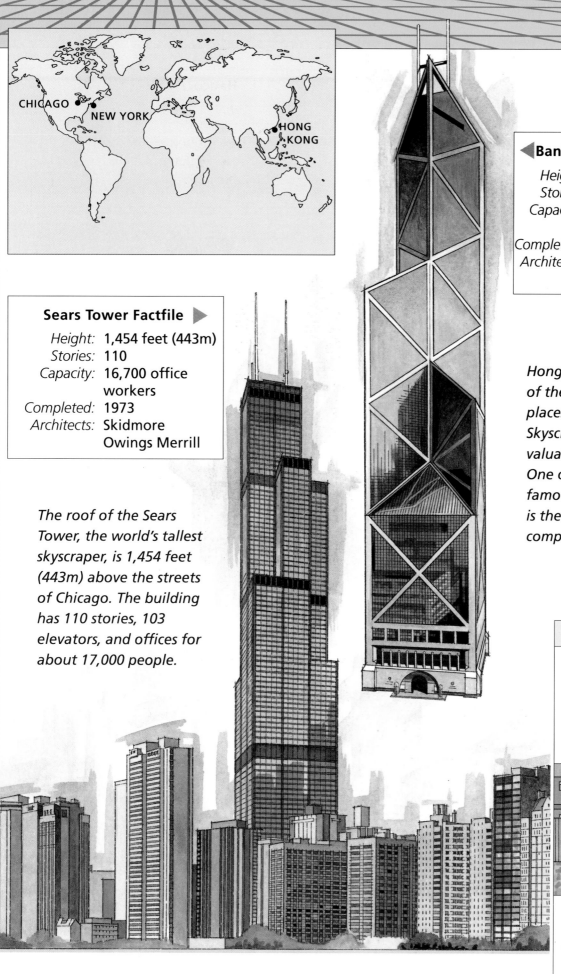

► Bank of China Factfile

Height: **1,200 feet (369m)**
Stories: **70**
Capacity: **6000 office workers**
Completed: **1990**
Architects: **I. M. Pei and Partners**

◄ Sears Tower Factfile

Height: **1,454 feet (443m)**
Stories: **110**
Capacity: **16,700 office workers**
Completed: **1973**
Architects: **Skidmore Owings Merrill**

Hong Kong is one of the most crowded places in the world. Skyscrapers provide valuable extra space. One of Hong Kong's famous skyscrapers is the Bank of China, completed in 1990.

The roof of the Sears Tower, the world's tallest skyscraper, is 1,454 feet (443m) above the streets of Chicago. The building has 110 stories, 103 elevators, and offices for about 17,000 people.

STEP BY STEP

In this space on each double page we show you a stage in the building of an imaginary skyscraper. The sequence starts here and ends on page 27.

1 Construction workers must clear away all the old buildings on a site before work on a new skyscraper can begin.

5

Inside a Skyscraper

If you could take a skyscraper apart, you would see that it is a complicated building with millions of parts. On these two pages, you can discover the different sections of a skyscraper. Then look at the following pages to find out more about each one.

The simple surface of this skyscraper hides millions of different parts.

The framework

A skyscraper's **framework** holds up all the other parts of the skyscraper, such as the walls and floors. It is like your skeleton, which supports your muscles and organs. Skyscraper frames are normally steel or concrete.

The strong frame of a skyscraper holds up the entire building.

STEEL FRAME

FRAME RESTS ON FOUNDATIONS

Foundations reach deep into the ground to support the skyscraper.

SOIL

BASEMENT

FOUNDATIONS REST ON BEDROCK

A firm footing

The skyscraper framework needs solid foundations to keep it firmly rooted in the ground and keep it from tipping over. Foundations are always the first part of a skyscraper to be built. But, when the building is complete, they are hidden underground.

Walls and floors

The tallest skyscrapers have more than 100 stories. The floor of each one is made from a very wide, flat piece of concrete, which is supported by the skyscraper's framework. The outer walls of a skyscraper hang on the outside beams and columns of the framework. Ordinary buildings, such as houses, work the other way around—the outside walls support the rest of the structure.

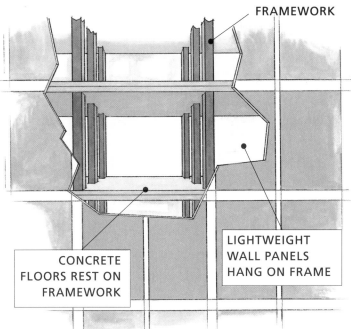

FRAMEWORK

CONCRETE FLOORS REST ON FRAMEWORK

LIGHTWEIGHT WALL PANELS HANG ON FRAME

Walls and floors are gradually added to the skyscraper as its framework grows upward.

Skyscraper services

A skyscraper needs the same services as an ordinary house. These include electricity, water, waste disposal, and telephones and communications. In a house, the services are supplied to one or two stories. But in a skyscraper they have to be supplied to many different stories, some of them hundreds of feet above the ground.

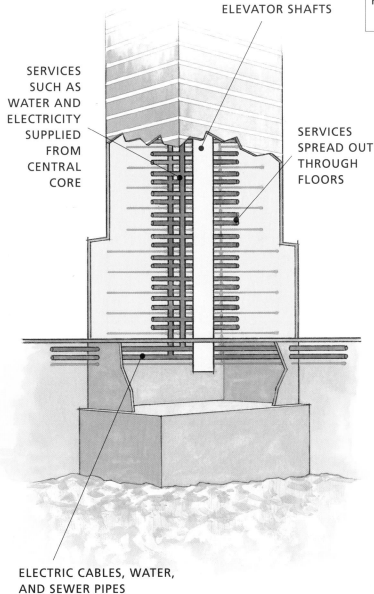

ELEVATOR SHAFTS

SERVICES SUCH AS WATER AND ELECTRICITY SUPPLIED FROM CENTRAL CORE

SERVICES SPREAD OUT THROUGH FLOORS

ELECTRIC CABLES, WATER, AND SEWER PIPES

Services such as electricity and water are supplied to all the stories of a skyscraper from a central core.

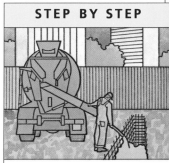

STEP BY STEP

2 A trench is dug around the site and filled with concrete. This **retaining wall** stops earth movements affecting other buildings.

7

Under the Ground

Hidden away underneath the ground floor of a skyscraper is one of its most important parts—the foundations. A large skyscraper weighs hundreds of thousands of tons. It needs strong foundations to keep it steady and stop it from sinking into the ground.

Surveying the ground

The type of foundations a building has depends on the geology—the type of soil and rock—of the ground. A geological survey is always carried out before the foundations are designed. It may find solid rock, layers of different rocks, or soft soil.

Foundations go very deep. A 650-foot- (200m-) high sky- scraper may have piles (see opposite) reaching a quarter of its height, into the ground.

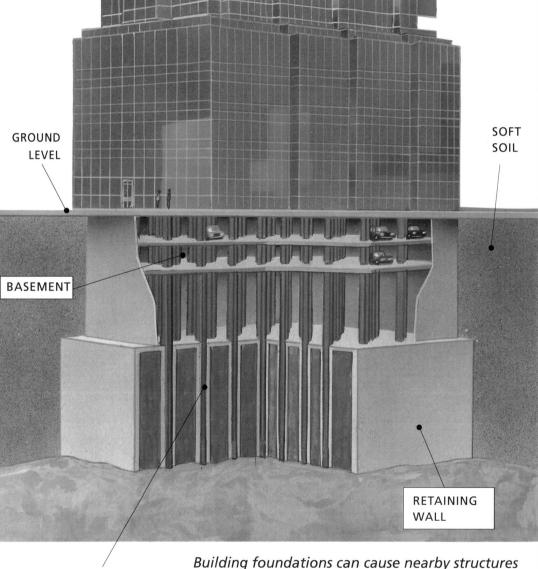

GROUND LEVEL

SOFT SOIL

BASEMENT

RETAINING WALL

PILE FOUNDATIONS REACH DOWN TO SOLID ROCK

Building foundations can cause nearby structures to move. So builders often dig a trench around the site and fill it with concrete. This makes a barrier called a retaining wall that helps to keep earth movements from traveling beyond the site.

Piles or rafts?

If the survey discovers solid rock near the surface, the foundations rest on top of the rock. If the solid rock is deeper down, under soil, long steel or concrete columns are driven into the ground to reach it. These columns are called **piles**. Where there is deep, soft soil, special foundations are needed to spread the building's weight. These prevent the ground from sagging under the skyscraper. One method of constructing these foundations is to build a huge concrete slab, called a **raft**, on which the building "floats."

The Citicorp Center in New York is supported by four huge columns. Under each column are piles reaching deep into the ground.

COLUMNS

STEEL PILES SUPPORT EACH COLUMN

The terminal of Kansai Airport in Japan, which opened in 1994, is supported by hydraulic jacks.

Settling

It is normal for the foundations of a skyscraper to move slightly as the ground settles under them. But if one part of the foundations moves more than another, the building's frame can become twisted. The new Kansai International Airport in Osaka Bay, Japan was built on a specially constructed island. Engineers installed **hydraulic jacks**, special devices for lifting heavy weights, under each column of the airport terminal building. Computers are used to measure how much the ground settles and automatically adjust the jacks to keep the new building in shape.

STEP BY STEP

3 A machine called a **pile driver** pounds metal piles into the ground to make the skyscraper's strong, deep foundations.

Steel Frames

A skyscraper's steel frame is made by joining together long, thin sections of steel. The vertical sections that go from the ground to the top of the frame are called columns. The horizontal sections between the columns are called beams. The columns support the beams, and the beams support the skyscraper's floors, everything on the floors, and the walls. The bases of the columns are attached to the foundations. All the sections are made before any building work starts. Then they are welded and connected on-site like a huge jigsaw puzzle.

A skyscraper's frame is made of vertical columns and horizontal beams.

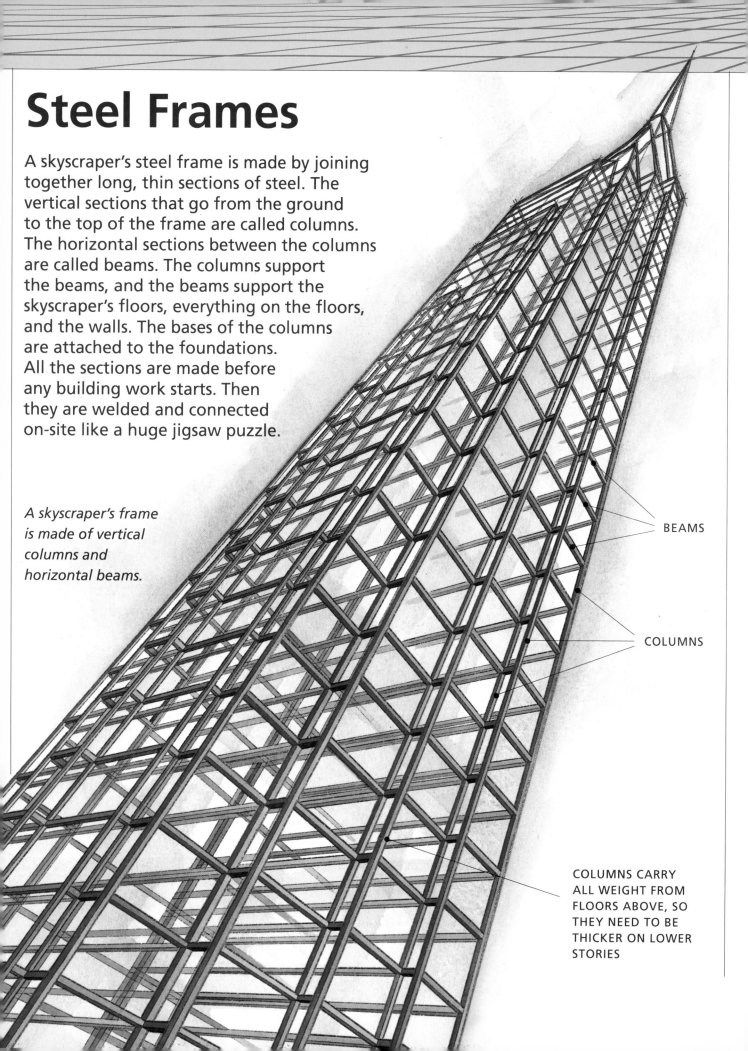

BEAMS

COLUMNS

COLUMNS CARRY ALL WEIGHT FROM FLOORS ABOVE, SO THEY NEED TO BE THICKER ON LOWER STORIES

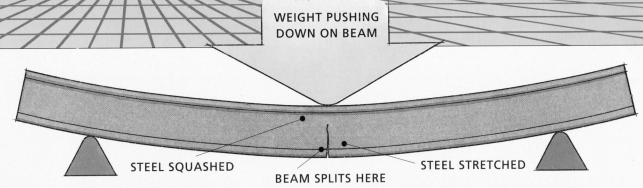

WEIGHT PUSHING DOWN ON BEAM

STEEL SQUASHED

BEAM SPLITS HERE

STEEL STRETCHED

Bending beams

When you put weight on a steel beam, the beam bends downward. As it bends, the steel in the top of the beam is squashed (this is called compression), and the steel in the bottom is stretched (this is called tension). If the steel in the bottom of the beam is stretched too much, it breaks, and the beam collapses. To prevent this, beams are made in special shapes that keep them from bending too far. A beam 16 feet (5m) long and about 12 inches (30cm) high, made with steel about 1 inch (3cm) thick, could support ten family-sized cars.

Beam shapes

There are several different shapes of beams, as you can see if you look at them from the end.

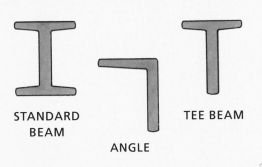

STANDARD BEAM

ANGLE

TEE BEAM

Beams are designed to be light and strong. Beams must be light to reduce the weight pressing down on columns. Light beams provide more steel where it is needed, without extra weight.

HIGH-STRENGTH STEEL BOLTS

Column shapes

If you look at the end of a steel column, you will see that its shape is different from the shape of a beam. The special H-shape keeps it from buckling under great weight from above. Steel columns may also be surrounded with concrete to help prevent buckling.

UNIVERSAL COLUMN

Joining up

The joints between sections of the frame need to be as strong as the sections themselves. They are designed at the same time as the beams and columns, and holes for **bolted joints** are drilled then, too. The sections are joined with strong bolts, or **welded** together by adding molten metal to the joints, then letting them cool.

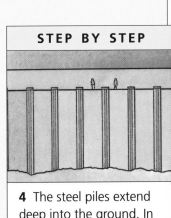

4 The steel piles extend deep into the ground. In some buildings, the basement will be built in the spaces between the piles.

Concrete Frames

Apart from steel, concrete is the only material widely used for building skyscraper frames. But it is not normally used for very tall skyscrapers because it is too heavy. Concrete is made by mixing small stones, cement, and water. After just a few hours, the mixture becomes hard. But it takes about a month to reach its full strength.

Strengths and weaknesses

An enormous force is needed to crush concrete. A concrete cube 3 feet (1m) wide could support ten full jumbo jets. But concrete is weak when it is stretched, and snaps quite easily. So thick, often coiled, steel wires are buried in the concrete in the places where it will be under the most stress. This strong concrete and steel mixture is called **reinforced concrete**.

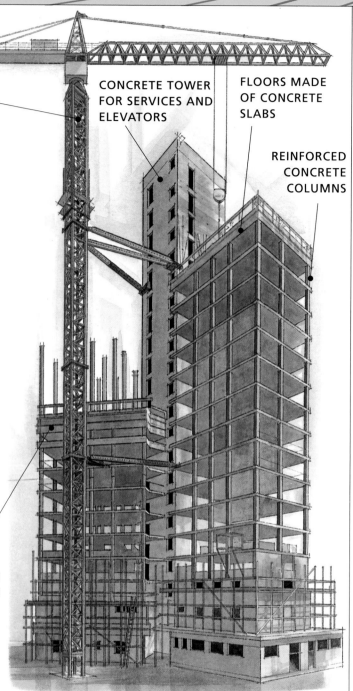

CONSTRUCTION CRANE

CONCRETE TOWER FOR SERVICES AND ELEVATORS

FLOORS MADE OF CONCRETE SLABS

REINFORCED CONCRETE COLUMNS

FLOOR SLABS WAITING TO BE LIFTED INTO PLACE

Simple concrete frames like this one are used for low-rise skyscrapers. These are 30 stories or less and often divided into small rooms.

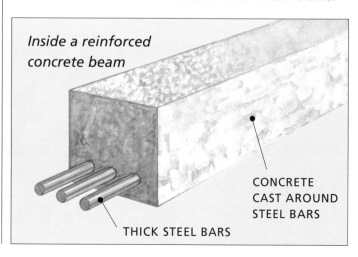

Inside a reinforced concrete beam

CONCRETE CAST AROUND STEEL BARS

THICK STEEL BARS

Molding concrete

Concrete is liquid when it is mixed, so it can be poured into a mold and left to harden. This means that concrete can give a building not only its strength, but its shape, too. **Precast concrete** is made into sections away from the building site. The sections are then joined together on-site, in a similar way to a steel frame.

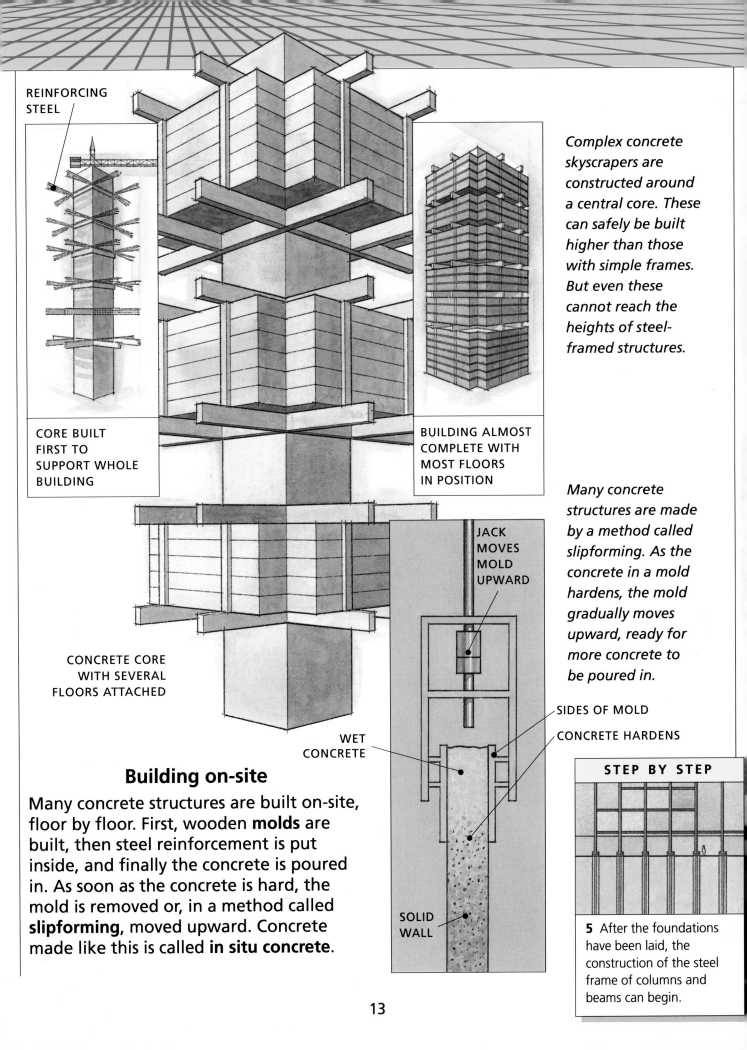

REINFORCING STEEL

CORE BUILT FIRST TO SUPPORT WHOLE BUILDING

BUILDING ALMOST COMPLETE WITH MOST FLOORS IN POSITION

CONCRETE CORE WITH SEVERAL FLOORS ATTACHED

Complex concrete skyscrapers are constructed around a central core. These can safely be built higher than those with simple frames. But even these cannot reach the heights of steel-framed structures.

Many concrete structures are made by a method called slipforming. As the concrete in a mold hardens, the mold gradually moves upward, ready for more concrete to be poured in.

JACK MOVES MOLD UPWARD

SIDES OF MOLD

CONCRETE HARDENS

WET CONCRETE

SOLID WALL

Building on-site

Many concrete structures are built on-site, floor by floor. First, wooden **molds** are built, then steel reinforcement is put inside, and finally the concrete is poured in. As soon as the concrete is hard, the mold is removed or, in a method called **slipforming**, moved upward. Concrete made like this is called **in situ concrete**.

STEP BY STEP

5 After the foundations have been laid, the construction of the steel frame of columns and beams can begin.

Floors and Walls

A skyscraper's floors and walls are supported by the beams and columns in its frame. Every skyscraper floor is made from a thick sheet of concrete, but steel-framed skyscrapers and concrete-framed skyscrapers use sheets of different shapes. The heavy outside walls of a skyscraper hang on the frame. The inside walls are light and thin, and stand on the floor.

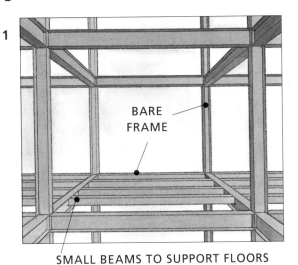

BARE FRAME

SMALL BEAMS TO SUPPORT FLOORS

1 *The bare frame of a steel skyscraper forms the base for its floors. These are added story by story as the building rises from the ground.*

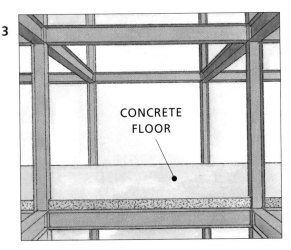

CONCRETE FLOOR

STEEL DECKING REINFORCES SET CONCRETE

Pouring floors

The floors of a steel-framed skyscraper rest on the beams in the frame. They are made by laying thin sheets of steel, called **decking**, side by side, then pouring concrete on top. The concrete is carefully leveled before it hardens, to give a smooth floor. In concrete-framed buildings, the floors themselves are part of the structure. Each floor is really a very wide concrete beam, so the floors do not need separate beams to support their edges.

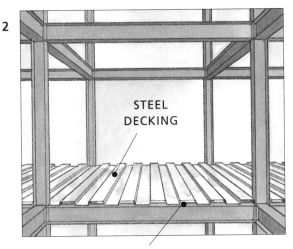

STEEL DECKING

DECKING ATTACHED TO FRAME WITH BOLTS

2 *To make a floor, steel decking is fixed across the beams. The U-shapes in the decking help to keep it from bending when heavy concrete is poured on.*

3 *Once the decking is in position, construction workers cover it with concrete. While the concrete is still wet, the workers smooth it so that the floor dries completely flat.*

Hanging walls

A skyscraper's outside wall is called the cladding or the **curtain wall**. The cladding keeps the inside of the building warm, dry, quiet, and clean. Many different materials, such as glass, aluminum, steel, brick, and polished stone are used for cladding. Metal or stone cladding is made in thin sheets to keep it as light as possible. The building's frame has to support these outside walls. The choice of cladding is important because it is the only part of a skyscraper that most people see. It gives the skyscraper its own special look.

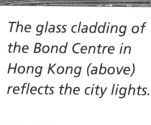

The twin towers of the World Trade Center in New York (above) are covered in aluminum cladding that gives them a metallic sheen.

The glass cladding of the Bond Centre in Hong Kong (above) reflects the city lights.

The Messeturm (Exhibition Tower) in Frankfurt, Germany (left), has red granite cladding that gives the tower strength and color.

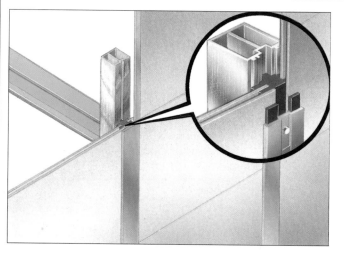

In some areas of the world where earthquakes are common, for example in Japan and on the West Coast of the U.S., glass cladding is attached to buildings with rubber channels. The glass can then move around without cracking as the building shakes.

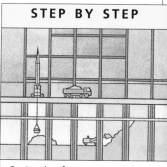

6 As the frame rises, builders begin to construct the basement. This is protected by the retaining wall, which is waterproof.

Fixtures and Fittings

A skyscraper would be useless without fixtures and fittings, so architects and engineers make careful plans for these. Every story needs services such as heating, air-conditioning, plumbing for toilets and kitchens, electricity for lighting and for machines such as computers, and many telephone lines. Easy access to elevators and stairs is also essential.

The central core

Most skyscrapers have a central core that runs all the way from the basement to the top story. It contains hot and cold water pipes, heating and air-conditioning ducts, electric cables, elevator shafts and stairwells. The pipes, ducts, and cables branch out at each floor. Hundreds of miles (km) of cables and pipes are needed.

The importance of elevators

Imagine a skyscraper without elevators. If you worked at the top of a 100-story skyscraper, you would spend about an hour every day walking up and down stairs! An elevator, on the other hand, travels up and down in a couple of minutes.

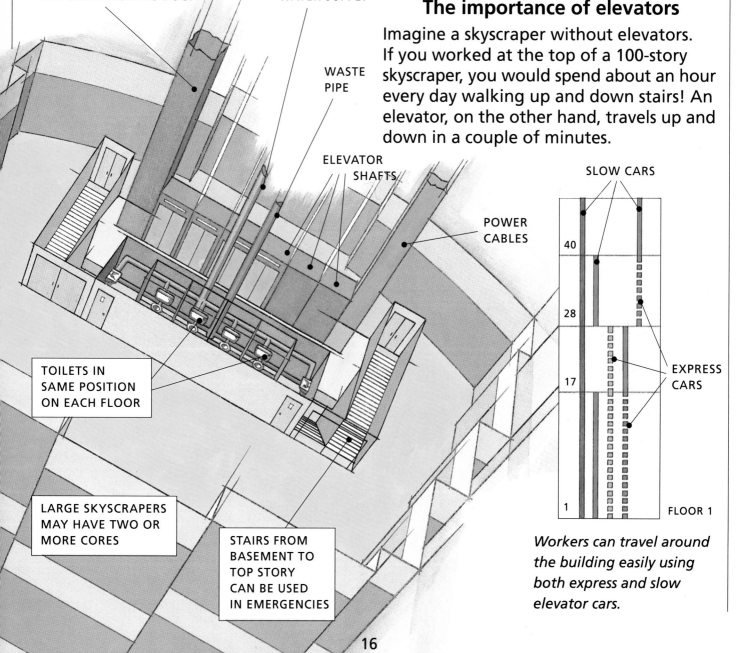

AIR-CONDITIONING DUCT

WATER SUPPLY

WASTE PIPE

ELEVATOR SHAFTS

POWER CABLES

TOILETS IN SAME POSITION ON EACH FLOOR

LARGE SKYSCRAPERS MAY HAVE TWO OR MORE CORES

STAIRS FROM BASEMENT TO TOP STORY CAN BE USED IN EMERGENCIES

SLOW CARS

EXPRESS CARS

40

28

17

1

FLOOR 1

Workers can travel around the building easily using both express and slow elevator cars.

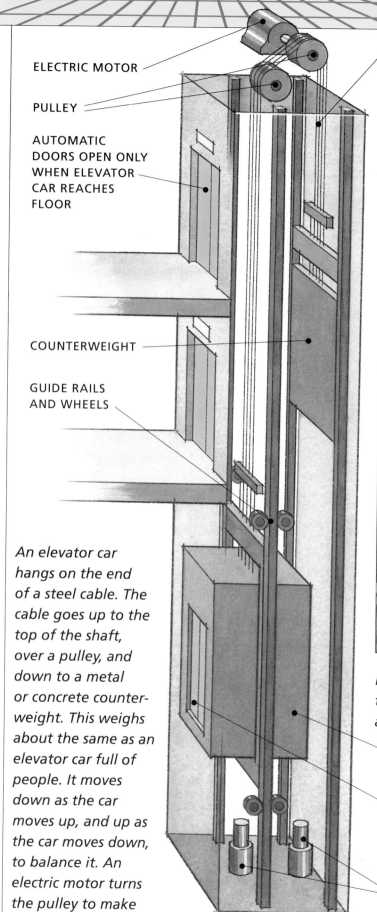

ELECTRIC MOTOR

PULLEY

AUTOMATIC DOORS OPEN ONLY WHEN ELEVATOR CAR REACHES FLOOR

COUNTERWEIGHT

GUIDE RAILS AND WHEELS

An elevator car hangs on the end of a steel cable. The cable goes up to the top of the shaft, over a pulley, and down to a metal or concrete counterweight. This weighs about the same as an elevator car full of people. It moves down as the car moves up, and up as the car moves down, to balance it. An electric motor turns the pulley to make the elevator move.

STEEL CABLE

Fast and slow

A big, modern skyscraper may have up to 30 elevator cars, but only one or two go all the way from top to bottom. Most are either slow cars that stop at each floor, or express cars that stop at every fifth or tenth floor. To reach a particular floor you may have to take an express, then a slow car. A computer controls all the cars. It detects people pressing the buttons and sends cars up and down so that passengers are moved efficiently. This is especially important when thousands of office workers are all arriving or leaving at once.

In modern skyscrapers, computers control the elevators, fire and security alarms, and air-conditioning.

ELEVATOR CAR

INTERNAL DOORS

PISTONS ABSORB ENERGY IF ELEVATOR FALLS TOO FAST

STEP BY STEP

7 Concrete is poured from a pump over bolted steel sheets, called decking, to make all the floors of the new skyscraper.

Skyscraper Design

Before building work can begin, every detail of a skyscraper must be designed. The design process starts when the owner, the person who is paying for the skyscraper to be built, hires an **architect**. The architect discusses with the owner what the building will be used for, how much floor space is needed, and how much money there is to spend.

Looking good

Next the architect visits the skyscraper site and begins making sketches. He or she must design a building that meets the owner's needs, looks good, and fits in with existing buildings. This means deciding on the height and shape of the skyscraper and the sort of cladding it will have. It also means working out how the building will affect its surroundings, for example where its shadow will fall. The architect works with **structural engineers**. They help him to plan the foundations and the frame, which make up the building's basic structure. Gradually, the details of the new skyscraper are worked out, and drawings are made for every part.

*Architects often use **computer-aided design (CAD)** systems. All the details of a new building are entered into a computer. Using CAD systems, the architect can produce plans and drawings. These give architects and engineers a clear idea of what the final structure will look like.*

*Advanced CAD systems produce **virtual reality** designs that architects can view from any angle. This one shows the Schlumberger Scientific Research Centre in Cambridge, England.*

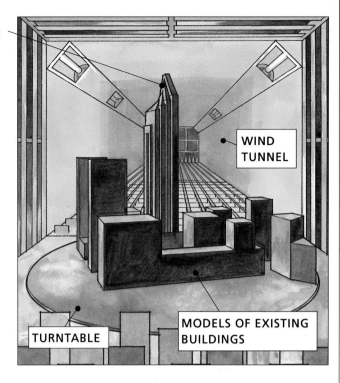

Dead or alive

Any structure must be built to withstand certain forces, called **loads**. Dead load is the weight of the building itself. Live load is the weight of everything in the building, including the people. Wind load is the force of the wind on the sides of the building. A structural engineer is the person who makes sure that the building will stand up. Information about the structure, such as the length of the beams and columns, is stored on computer. Using the computer the architect works out how strong each part needs to be to resist the loads. It can also work out how much the skyscraper will sway in strong winds.

WIND TUNNEL

TURNTABLE

MODELS OF EXISTING BUILDINGS

Architects can "walk through" a three-dimensional virtual reality interior like this one. In fact it only exists in the memory of a computer.

Even a computer finds it difficult to predict exactly how wind will affect a new building. So sometimes a scale model of the building is tested on a turntable inside a wind tunnel. A powerful fan at the end of the tunnel can blow air along it at up to 131 feet (40m) per second.

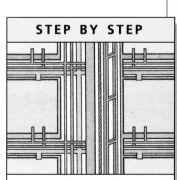

STEP BY STEP

8 Electricity, water supply, and other services are added to the central core of the building as the steel framework grows.

Safety and Comfort

During a working day there may be thousands of people inside a skyscraper. One of the design team's most important jobs is to make sure that they are safe and comfortable. The main danger in a skyscraper is fire. If it starts low in the building, it can trap people in the upper floors, where rescue services cannot easily reach them. Earthquakes and high winds are also possible problems.

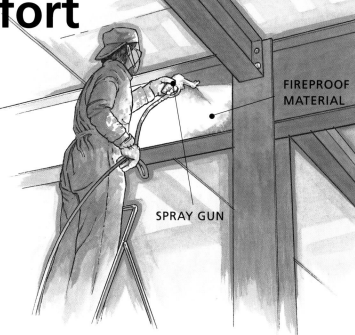

Spraying steel columns and beams with fireproof material or paint reduces the risk of buckling.

Fire safety

Skyscrapers are equipped with special fire alarm systems. Electronic **sensors** on every floor automatically sound the fire alarm and set off water sprinklers if they detect smoke. Some skyscrapers also have **pressurization systems**. When a fire alarm goes off, they increase the air pressure in escape routes (corridors and stairwells). This makes it harder for smoke to escape from burning rooms.

Sprinkler heads automatically release a spray of water when smoke is detected in a room.

Fireproofing

The steel and concrete structure of a building cannot burn, but the fierce heat of a fire can make the steel buckle. During construction, the steel beams and columns are sprayed or covered with fireproof material to help prevent this. Special fireproof paints may also be used.

Steel beams treated with fireproof material are tested at different temperatures in a furnace to see exactly how they will react in a fire.

84°F (29°C)

388°F (198°C)

518°F (270°C)

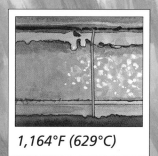

1,164°F (629°C)

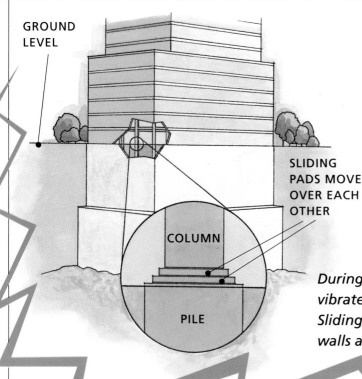

GROUND LEVEL

COLUMN

SLIDING PADS MOVE OVER EACH OTHER

PILE

Earthquake protection

In an earthquake, the base of a building is shaken from side to side. Buildings that can bend and sway as the ground moves are less likely to be damaged than fixed buildings. Skyscrapers with steel or concrete frames move quite well. To help them move better still, engineers may put sliding pads or flexible rubber pads between the buildings and the ground.

During an earthquake, a building's foundations vibrate from side to side with the ground. Sliding pads reduce the vibrations passed on to walls and floors. This helps to prevent damage.

Swaying in the wind

In strong winds, the top of a skyscraper can sway from side to side by over three feet (1m). This does not harm the building, but it can make people on the top stories feel very sick! One way to lessen the effect of the wind is to strengthen the frame with diagonal steel sections. This is called **bracing**. The extra sections carry the wind load down to the ground so that the building sways less.

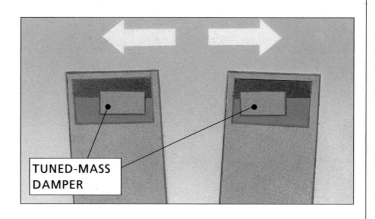

TUNED-MASS DAMPER

Mass dampers

A device called a **tuned-mass damper** is another way of preventing sway. A computer detects how far wind is making a building move in one direction, then moves a huge weight, the damper, at the top of the skyscraper in the other direction. This helps the swaying building return to a vertical position.

A tuned-mass damper is a hanging weight. As strong winds push a skyscraper one way, it swings the other way. The two opposite movements cancel each other out, so that the skyscraper stays relatively still.

STEP BY STEP

9 Once the frame is nearly complete, builders begin to attach the cladding – the exterior walls – to lower floors.

Beginning to Build

As soon as the architect, engineers, and owners have completed and approved the design of a skyscraper, building can begin.

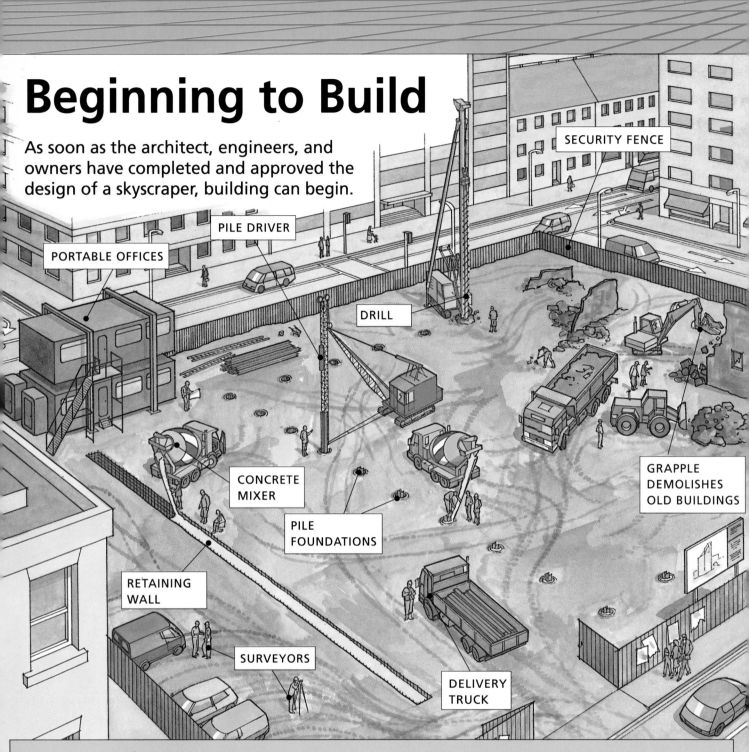

PILE DRIVER

SECURITY FENCE

PORTABLE OFFICES

DRILL

GRAPPLE DEMOLISHES OLD BUILDINGS

CONCRETE MIXER

PILE FOUNDATIONS

RETAINING WALL

SURVEYORS

DELIVERY TRUCK

Clearing a space

The first job on a construction site is to demolish existing buildings and clear away all the rubble and rubbish. When there is a clear space, a building company, called the **main contractor,** can move in. This company is in charge of the site. It organizes **subcontractors,** such as plumbers and electricians, and **suppliers,** who provide the materials. Then, working from the architect's plans, **surveyors** carry out a process called **laying out.** This means measuring where the building's foundations should go. Construction of the foundations can then begin. At the same time, suppliers make parts for later use. They may be many thousands of miles away from the building site.

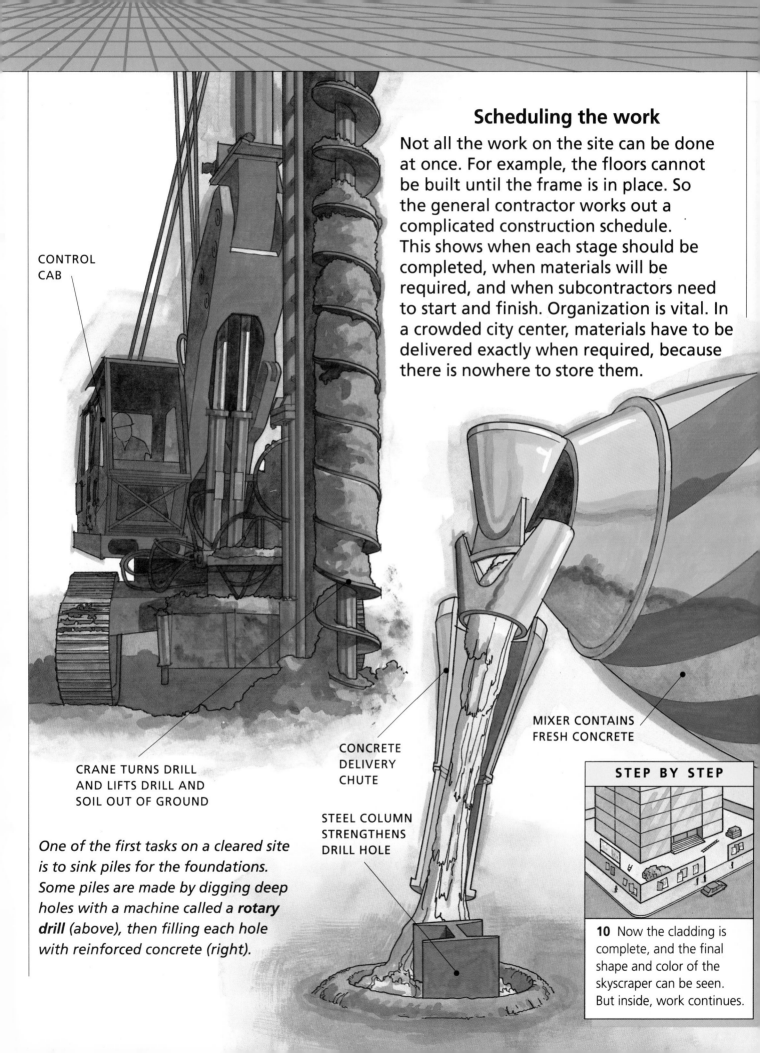

CONTROL
CAB

Scheduling the work

Not all the work on the site can be done at once. For example, the floors cannot be built until the frame is in place. So the general contractor works out a complicated construction schedule. This shows when each stage should be completed, when materials will be required, and when subcontractors need to start and finish. Organization is vital. In a crowded city center, materials have to be delivered exactly when required, because there is nowhere to store them.

MIXER CONTAINS
FRESH CONCRETE

CRANE TURNS DRILL
AND LIFTS DRILL AND
SOIL OUT OF GROUND

CONCRETE
DELIVERY
CHUTE

STEEL COLUMN
STRENGTHENS
DRILL HOLE

*One of the first tasks on a cleared site is to sink piles for the foundations. Some piles are made by digging deep holes with a machine called a **rotary drill** (above), then filling each hole with reinforced concrete (right).*

STEP BY STEP

10 Now the cladding is complete, and the final shape and color of the skyscraper can be seen. But inside, work continues.

Building Frames and Floors

Once the foundations are complete, work begins on the skyscraper's steel frame. As it rises above the ground, concrete floors are added to the lower stories.

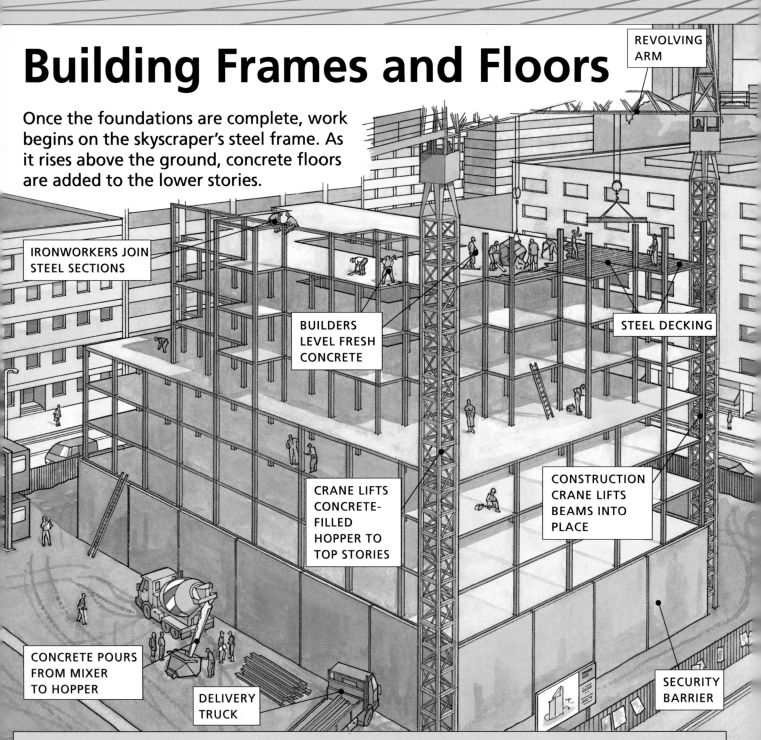

REVOLVING ARM

IRONWORKERS JOIN STEEL SECTIONS

BUILDERS LEVEL FRESH CONCRETE

STEEL DECKING

CRANE LIFTS CONCRETE-FILLED HOPPER TO TOP STORIES

CONSTRUCTION CRANE LIFTS BEAMS INTO PLACE

CONCRETE POURS FROM MIXER TO HOPPER

DELIVERY TRUCK

SECURITY BARRIER

Beams and columns

The beams and sections of the columns are delivered to the site exactly when they are needed. Each piece is carefully numbered so that the people who build the frame (called **ironworkers**) can match them to the plans. Delivering the pieces at the right time is essential. If they arrive before the ironworkers are ready, the delivery trucks get in the way. If they are late, the ironworkers have nothing to do. Giant construction cranes lift the heavy steel pieces from the trucks to where they are needed. Here they are immediately welded into place or bolted together with high-strength bolts.

Adding floors

Gradually the skyscraper's frame rises from the ground. When a few stories of the frame are complete, work begins on the bottom floors. First, steel decking is laid down and fixed to the beams with bolts. Next, concrete is poured over the decking. The concrete is lifted to the floor in a large **hopper** and sometimes pumped to where it is needed by concrete pumps. Before it hardens, the concrete is carefully smoothed over. Holes are left in the floor for stairwells and elevator shafts.

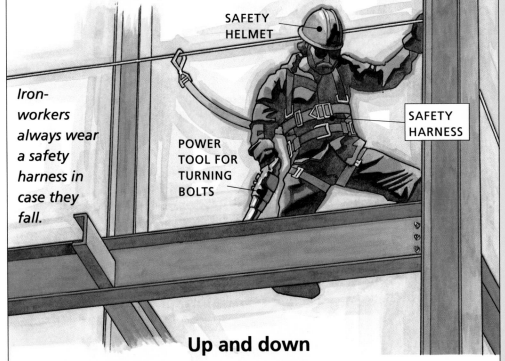

SAFETY HELMET

SAFETY HARNESS

POWER TOOL FOR TURNING BOLTS

Iron-workers always wear a safety harness in case they fall.

Up and down

As the frame and floors are built above ground, the basement is constructed below ground. Here there will be machinery, such as **generators** and boilers, and often a parking area. Basement floors are like those above ground but lined with waterproof walls.

Underground parking saves money because owners do not have to buy more land to build parking areas.

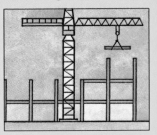

1 *A construction crane begins its work at ground level.*

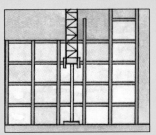

2 *The crane moves up to a new level on a hydraulic jack.*

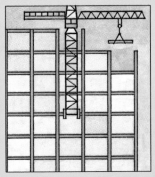

3 *Once in its new position, the crane is bolted to the frame.*

STEP BY STEP

11 Inside the finished skyscraper, subcontractors are working hard to put the finishing touches to services and decor.

Finishing Touches

As construction draws to a close, the skyscraper site is a scene of frantic activity. Inside, plumbers, electricians, engineers, and decorators are busy completing the new building.

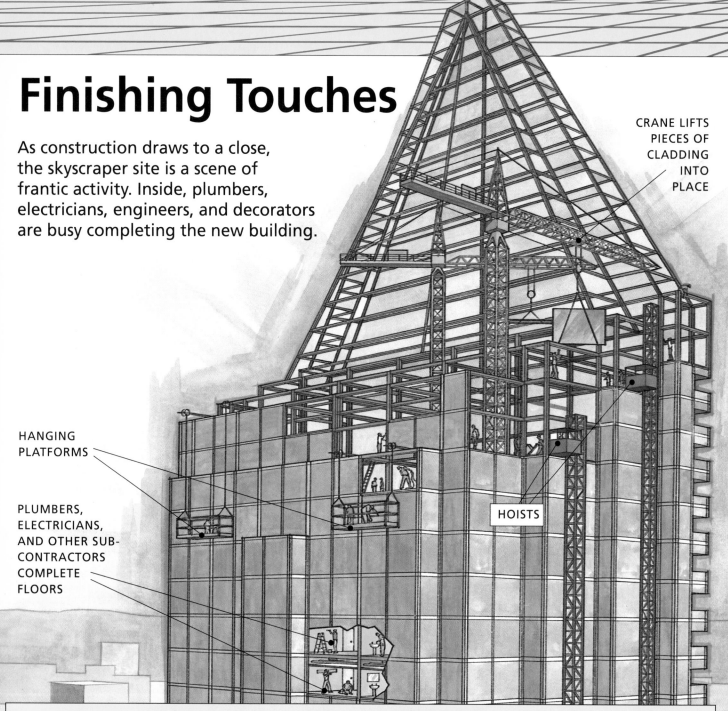

CRANE LIFTS PIECES OF CLADDING INTO PLACE

HANGING PLATFORMS

PLUMBERS, ELECTRICIANS, AND OTHER SUB-CONTRACTORS COMPLETE FLOORS

HOISTS

COMPLETED FLOORS

Finishing off

When some of the skyscraper's floors are completed, work can begin on the cladding. It is made off-site, then delivered in pieces and lifted into place. People working on platforms hanging on the outside of the building attach the cladding to the frame. But before it is finally attached, the steel frame is sprayed with a fireproof coating. There is a ceremony called topping out as the last piece of the frame is lifted carefully into place. As soon as the walls of one floor are complete, work starts inside the building. Subcontractors, including plumbers, electricians, heating, ventilation, and elevator engineers, fit their pipes, wires, and ducts in the core and under floors. Workers and materials are carried up in temporary lifts called **hoists** on the outside of the building. Work starts on ceilings, inside walls, toilets, and doors.

Finished at last

The final stage of the construction process is the decoration. After painting and wallpapering is done, carpet is laid on the floors. The structure of the skyscraper and the jumble of pipes and ducts are all hidden from view. Finally, all the working parts of the building are checked to make sure they work properly. At last, the builders leave the site, and the skyscraper is ready to hand over to the owner.

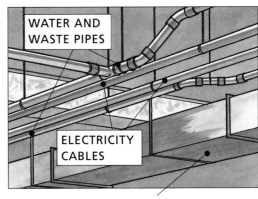

WATER AND WASTE PIPES

ELECTRICITY CABLES

AIR-CONDITIONING DUCT

Pipes, ducts, and cables are hidden by false ceilings. These are suspended on wires under the floors.

TOPMOST SECTION OF BUILDING

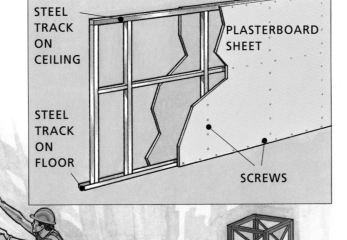

STEEL TRACK ON CEILING

PLASTERBOARD SHEET

STEEL TRACK ON FLOOR

SCREWS

*The inside walls of a skyscraper do not support anything. They simply divide the floors into rooms. To make the walls, metal frames called **studs** are fixed between the floors and ceilings. Thin sheets of plasterboard are attached to the studs with screws.*

The topping out ceremony is sometimes a great celebration. The final section is lowered into place, and the owner and architect come to the site and shake hands.

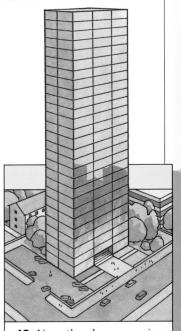

12 Now the skyscraper is finished, complete with gardens and parking areas. The architect's vision has become reality.

Towers and Masts

What is the difference between a skyscraper, a tower, and a mast? Towers and masts are not usually made up of stories like skyscrapers. Their job is often to hold something, such as a television transmission antenna, high in the air. Some are also built as monuments. Towers are freestanding structures, but masts are supported by guy wires. Usually towers and masts have to support only their own weight, and resist winds, so they are thinner and lighter than skyscrapers of the same height.

TRANSMISSION MAST

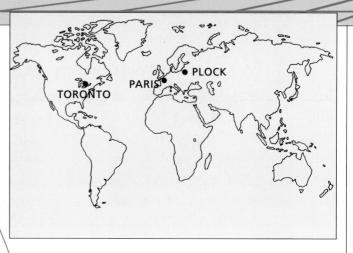

THE SPACE DECK IS 1,475 FEET (450M) ABOVE THE GROUND. ON A CLEAR DAY YOU CAN SEE OVER 93 MILES (150KM) FROM HERE.

THE SKY POD IS 1,150 FEET (350M) UP THE CN TOWER. ONE OF ITS SEVEN STORIES IS A REVOLVING RESTAURANT.

Height: 1,820 feet (555m)
Material: Concrete and steel
Use: Television transmission
Completed: 1975
Architects: John Andrews International

INSIDE THE MAST ARE TWO ELEVATORS AND AN EMERGENCY STAIRWELL

The CN Tower

The CN Tower in Toronto, Canada, is the tallest free-standing structure in the world. The tip of its television transmission antenna is 1,820 feet (555m) above the ground, and the complete structure weighs 130,000 tons.

Building the tower

The CN Tower was made by the slipforming method. Concrete was poured into a huge mold and left to harden. Then the mold was moved upward by hydraulic jacks and more concrete added. In this way, the tower grew over 10 feet (3m) a day. Although the tower is quite thin, the Y-shaped cross section makes it extremely stiff. The Sky Pod sways little, even in hurricane-force winds.

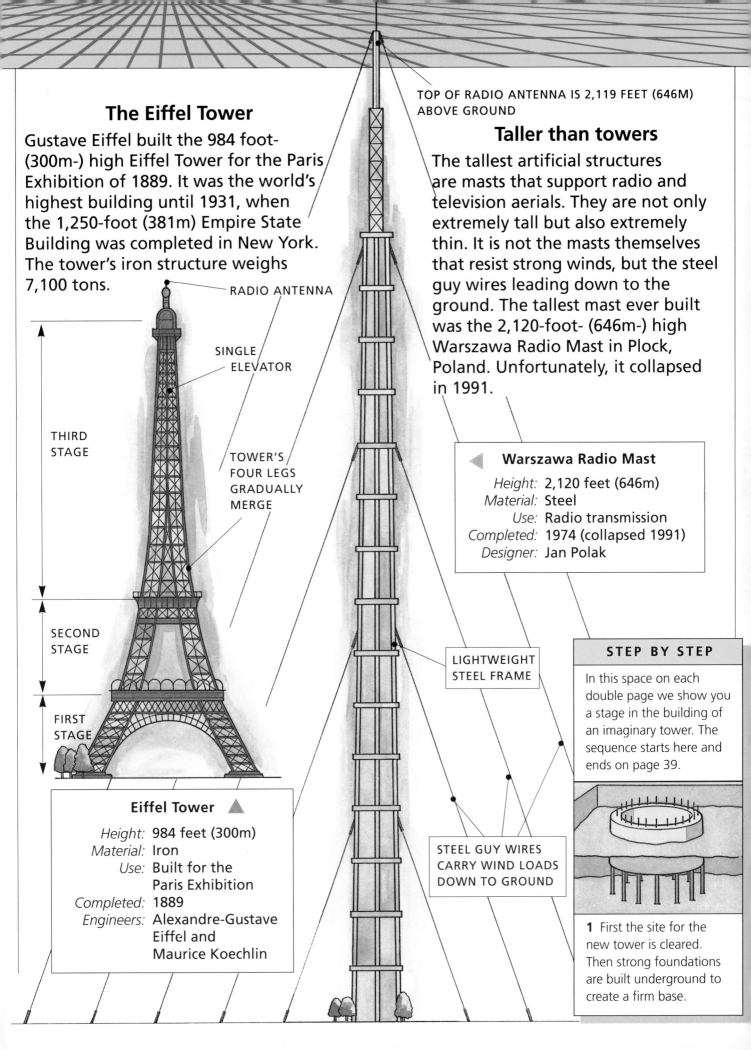

The Eiffel Tower

Gustave Eiffel built the 984 foot-(300m-) high Eiffel Tower for the Paris Exhibition of 1889. It was the world's highest building until 1931, when the 1,250-foot (381m) Empire State Building was completed in New York. The tower's iron structure weighs 7,100 tons.

RADIO ANTENNA

SINGLE ELEVATOR

TOWER'S FOUR LEGS GRADUALLY MERGE

THIRD STAGE

SECOND STAGE

FIRST STAGE

Eiffel Tower ▲

Height: 984 feet (300m)
Material: Iron
Use: Built for the Paris Exhibition
Completed: 1889
Engineers: Alexandre-Gustave Eiffel and Maurice Koechlin

TOP OF RADIO ANTENNA IS 2,119 FEET (646M) ABOVE GROUND

Taller than towers

The tallest artificial structures are masts that support radio and television aerials. They are not only extremely tall but also extremely thin. It is not the masts themselves that resist strong winds, but the steel guy wires leading down to the ground. The tallest mast ever built was the 2,120-foot- (646m-) high Warszawa Radio Mast in Plock, Poland. Unfortunately, it collapsed in 1991.

◄ Warszawa Radio Mast

Height: 2,120 feet (646m)
Material: Steel
Use: Radio transmission
Completed: 1974 (collapsed 1991)
Designer: Jan Polak

LIGHTWEIGHT STEEL FRAME

STEEL GUY WIRES CARRY WIND LOADS DOWN TO GROUND

STEP BY STEP

In this space on each double page we show you a stage in the building of an imaginary tower. The sequence starts here and ends on page 39.

1 First the site for the new tower is cleared. Then strong foundations are built underground to create a firm base.

Skyscrapers at Sea

Deep-water oil production platforms, also known as oil rigs, are the skyscrapers of the sea. They stand hundreds of miles from the shore. Some of them are in seas that would cover the top of even the tallest skyscrapers on land.

Towers and decks

Oil platforms have two main parts. Sitting on the seabed is a massive steel or concrete tower, made of four legs. Resting on top of the tower, above the waves, is a flat steel deck. On the deck are machinery for drilling into the seabed and removing the oil, and cranes for moving equipment and unloading supply ships. Here, too, are the quarters for the workers who live on the platform. There is also a helipad. This is where helicopters that fly workers on and off the rig can take off and land.

Building an oil platform

The tower and the deck of an oil production platform are built separately on land or in shallow, sheltered water. They may be joined together before being taken out to sea, or taken out separately and joined once they are in position. Steel towers are made in the same way as the steel frames of new skyscrapers, except that they lie on one side during construction. Some decks are built as one piece, others by joining together separate sections, called **modules**.

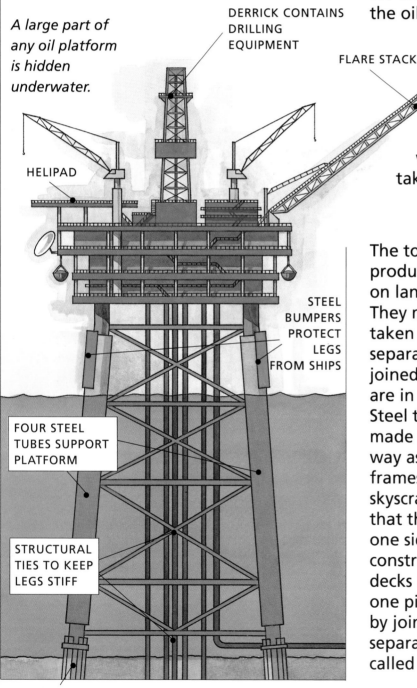

A large part of any oil platform is hidden underwater.

DERRICK CONTAINS DRILLING EQUIPMENT

FLARE STACK

HELIPAD

STEEL BUMPERS PROTECT LEGS FROM SHIPS

FOUR STEEL TUBES SUPPORT PLATFORM

STRUCTURAL TIES TO KEEP LEGS STIFF

PILES IN SEABED

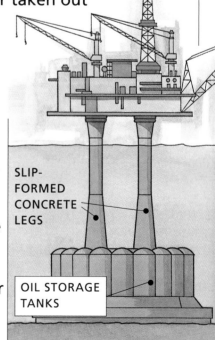

SLIP-FORMED CONCRETE LEGS

OIL STORAGE TANKS

Getting into place

When a rig is complete and the weather forecast is good, the platform is towed out to sea by tugs. When it is in the right place, the legs have to be sunk to the seabed. The tanks of a concrete rig are flooded with water, and the rig gradually sinks. Its massive weight, which can be nearly 1 million tons, keeps it in position, even in the worst storms. Steel rigs are anchored firmly to the seabed. If the deck modules are taken to the site separately, huge floating cranes lift them carefully into the correct place.

STEEL TUBES

A steel tower is towed out to sea on large floats. Deflating the floats in the right order tips the tower upright and makes it sink to the seabed.

Concrete platforms (far left) are only used in water over about 164 feet (50m) deep. They are held in place by their great weight. Concrete platforms cannot be used in very deep water because the pressure would crush the oil storage tanks.

Steel platforms (left) can be used in both shallow and deep water. They are held in place on the seabed by massive piles.

Concrete rig towers are built in shallow water, often in the fjords of Norway. A tower starts as a raft made of massive concrete tanks. Some of the tanks are built upward into tall towers by the slip-forming method.

STEP BY STEP

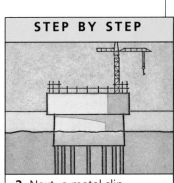

2 Next, a metal slip-forming frame is dropped over the foundations. Concrete is poured into the frame and left to dry.

Ancient High-Rises

The first real skyscrapers were built at the end of the nineteenth century, when steel became readily available. But they were not the first tall buildings. Since Ancient Egyptian times, people have tried to build tall structures. In the past, the main reason for building high was not to create more office space, but to get nearer to the gods and to their home in heaven.

The pyramids of Giza in Egypt were built using massive cut stone blocks.

Piles of stones

Without steel or reinforced concrete to make columns and beams, the only way of building high in ancient times was to pile stone blocks on top of one another. The Great Pyramid of Khufu in Giza, Egypt, was completed in about 2550 BC. It was originally 480 feet (146m) high and remained the tallest building in the world until the great cathedrals of the Middle Ages were built, 3,500 years later. The Great Pyramid kept the record for so long because much more advanced engineering skills were needed to build cathedrals' tall, thin towers. Unless great care is taken, the weight of the stone in the towers becomes so great that their bases collapse.

LIGHT MADE BY BURNING WOOD

HOLLOW TOWER

The Pharos of Alexandria

The first lighthouse

One of the tallest ancient structures was the Pharos of Alexandria, the world's first lighthouse. Built in about 270 BC on the island of Pharos, near Alexandria in Egypt, it was 400 feet (122m) high. The light was a bonfire on top of the tower, and wood for the fire was carried up a spiral ramp inside. Like many other stone structures in the city, the Pharos of Alexandria collapsed during an earthquake in the ninth century.

*In San'a, capital of Yemen, **tenements** have been made with mud bricks for over 1,000 years. Many are beautifully decorated, and some are ten stories high.*

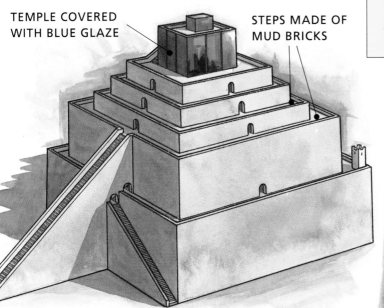

TEMPLE COVERED WITH BLUE GLAZE

STEPS MADE OF MUD BRICKS

The Tower of Babel. The temple on the top was dedicated to the Babylonian god Marduk.

The Tower of Babel

The Tower of Babel is described in Genesis, the first book of the Bible. According to this account, it was built in Babylonia, modern-day Iraq, in about 600 BC. The descendants of Noah, who constructed the tower, hoped that they would be able to climb up it to heaven. In reality, it was probably not a tower, but a 300-foot- (90m-) high stepped pyramid called a ziggurat.

The 180-foot- (55m-) high Leaning Tower of Pisa in Italy was built between 1174 and 1350. Unfortunately it was built on soft ground without proper foundations. As a result, the soil underneath has settled unevenly, making the tower lean about 16 feet (5m) toward the ground.

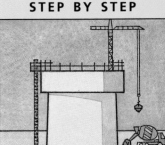

STEP BY STEP

3 The new concrete tower rises slowly from the ground as the massive slipforming machinery moves steadily upward.

The First Skyscrapers

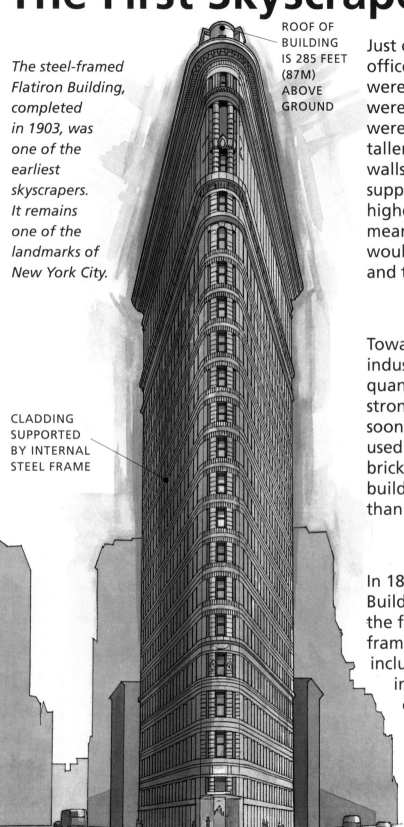

ROOF OF BUILDING IS 285 FEET (87M) ABOVE GROUND

The steel-framed Flatiron Building, completed in 1903, was one of the earliest skyscrapers. It remains one of the landmarks of New York City.

CLADDING SUPPORTED BY INTERNAL STEEL FRAME

Just over a hundred years ago, the tallest office buildings and apartment buildings were less than ten stories high. The floors were supported by wooden beams that were held up by stone or brick walls. The taller the building grew, the thicker the walls at the bottom needed to be to support the heavy walls above. Going higher than a few stories would have meant building massive walls. These would have been much too expensive, and too big for a crowded city.

Steel to the rescue

Toward the end of the nineteenth century, industry began to produce steel in large quantities. This new material was much stronger and lighter than stone. Builders soon realized that a steel frame could be used to support a building. Heavy stone or brick walls would no longer be needed, so buildings could have many more stories than ever before.

Going higher

In 1885, the ten-story Home Insurance Building in Chicago was finished. It was the first modern skyscraper. More steel-framed skyscrapers quickly followed, including the triangular Flatiron Building in New York. The first reinforced concrete skyscraper was the Ingalls Building in Cincinnati, which was built in 1903.

Up and up

Tall buildings would be useless without elevators. The first safe elevator was invented in 1852 by Elisha Otis, from Vermont. The elevator's automatic locking system prevented it from falling if the rope snapped. In 1857, the first Otis elevator was installed in a china shop in New York. It was powered by steam, and it moved at 39 feet (12m) a minute.

Faster and faster

The first modern electric elevator was in the Beaver Building in New York in 1903. The fastest elevators travel up and down the Yokohama Landmark Tower in Tokyo, Japan at 28 mph.

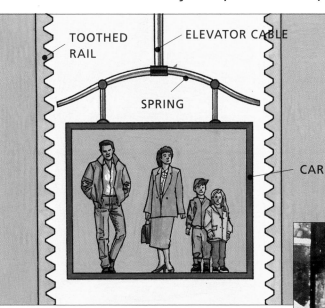

TOOTHED RAIL

ELEVATOR CABLE

SPRING

CAR

A simple elevator safety brake (above). In normal operation, the weight of the elevator car on the rope keeps the spring bent. If the rope breaks, the spring straightens, catching the toothed rail.

Elisha Otis demonstrated his elevator in New York in 1854 (right). The rope was deliberately cut to prove that the safety brake worked.

Within 20 years of the completion of the first skyscraper, work had started on the 60-story Woolworth Building in New York City.

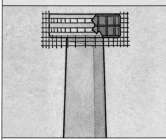

STEP BY STEP

4 When the tower is high enough, an observation platform is built. From here, people will be able to see far into the distance.

Higher and Higher

Since the first skyscrapers were constructed, people have tried to build them higher and higher. In crowded city centers, where land is expensive and scarce, every extra floor creates valuable space. In some cities, the plot of land on which a skyscraper stands is worth more money than the building itself. Also, there are always ambitious business people or city councils who want to be the owners of the tallest buildings in their city, country, or even the world.

Taller than ever

In theory, there is no reason why builders could not construct a skyscraper two or three times as high as the tallest ones in existence today. Structural engineers think they could design a frame strong enough to support a building such as the Millennium Tower (right). But there would be safety problems, especially in case of fire. How would the occupants be evacuated? And how would the firefighters put out a blaze right at the top?

A Japanese skyscraper, called the Millennium Tower, may be built in a lagoon 1 mile (2km) out to sea. It would be 2,625 feet (800m) high, with 150 stories of office and living space. The structure would be supported by a steel core and an external steel frame.

COMMUNICATIONS PYLON

CENTRAL STEEL CORE

150 STORIES OF STORES, HOMES, AND OFFICES

STEEL SPIRALS ON OUTSIDE OF BUILDING FORM VERY STRONG TUBE STRUCTURE

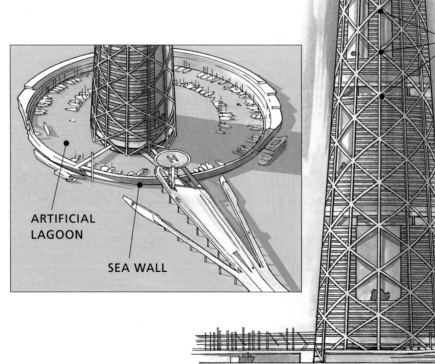

ARTIFICIAL LAGOON

SEA WALL

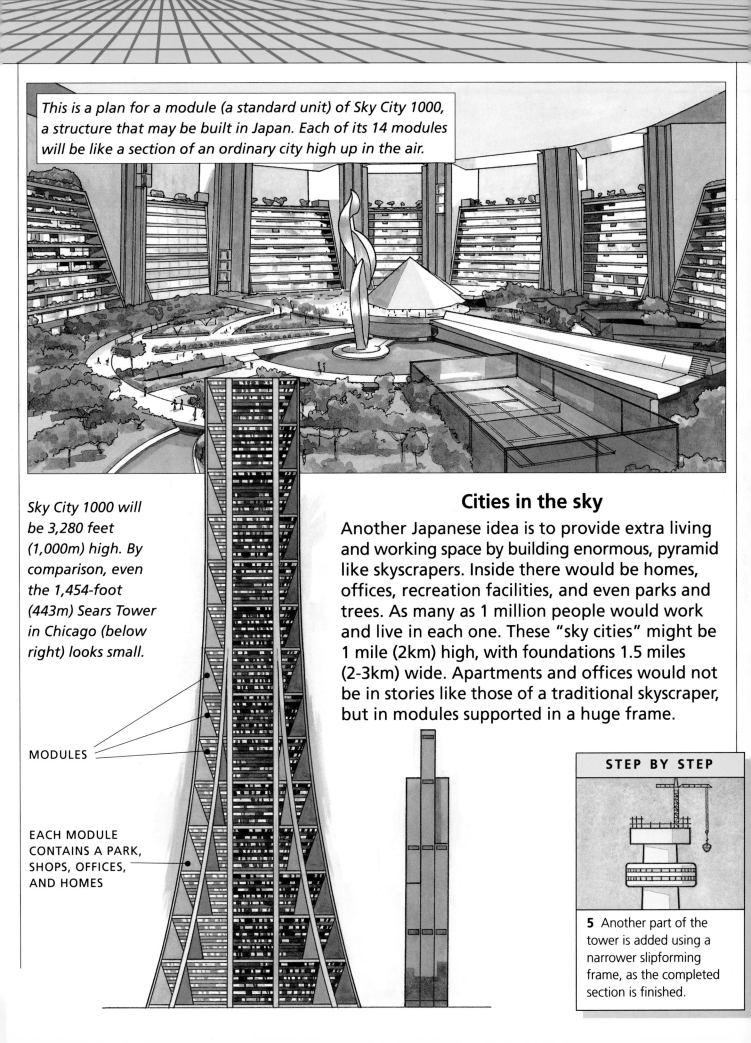

This is a plan for a module (a standard unit) of Sky City 1000, a structure that may be built in Japan. Each of its 14 modules will be like a section of an ordinary city high up in the air.

Sky City 1000 will be 3,280 feet (1,000m) high. By comparison, even the 1,454-foot (443m) Sears Tower in Chicago (below right) looks small.

MODULES

EACH MODULE CONTAINS A PARK, SHOPS, OFFICES, AND HOMES

Cities in the sky

Another Japanese idea is to provide extra living and working space by building enormous, pyramid like skyscrapers. Inside there would be homes, offices, recreation facilities, and even parks and trees. As many as 1 million people would work and live in each one. These "sky cities" might be 1 mile (2km) high, with foundations 1.5 miles (2-3km) wide. Apartments and offices would not be in stories like those of a traditional skyscraper, but in modules supported in a huge frame.

STEP BY STEP

5 Another part of the tower is added using a narrower slipforming frame, as the completed section is finished.

Skyscraper Architecture

Architectural styles have changed many times throughout history, and they are still changing today. Different styles may have grown out of new engineering techniques, such as arch-building, or a new material, such as reinforced concrete. These developments make new and different ways of building possible. Even the relatively short history of skyscrapers has seen many changes.

Art deco

Shining stainless steel and glass arches make the Chrysler Building one of the most famous landmarks in New York City. It was designed by William Van Alen and built during the late 1920s, in a style called **art deco**. The outside is decorated with symbols that also appeared on the Chrysler cars of that time. Other skyscrapers in New York, such as the Woolworth Building and the Empire State Building, were built in a similar, stepped style.

CHRYSLER SYMBOLS

STAINLESS STEEL AND GLASS CLADDING

EAGLES MATCH CHRYSLER CAR HOOD ORNAMENT

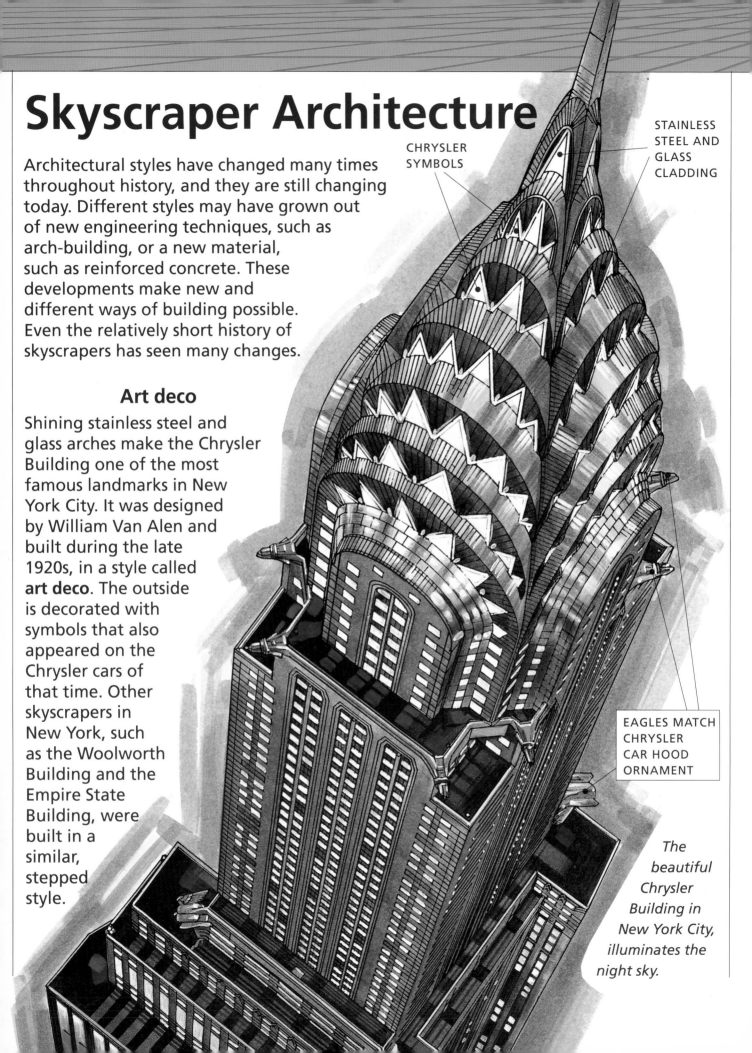

The beautiful Chrysler Building in New York City, illuminates the night sky.

Frank Lloyd Wright

Frank Lloyd Wright (1869-1959) was a famous American architect. His designs included one used for the Guggenheim Museum in New York. He also drew up plans for a needle-like, "mile-high" skyscraper (in fact, just over 5,250 feet (1,600m) tall). If it had been built, it would have been over three times as high as the world's tallest building, the Sears Tower in Chicago.

Glass and concrete

Most modern skyscrapers have a fairly simple design. The cladding is often concrete and glass, which reflects the sky and gives a sleek, dark appearance.

The Seagram Building in New York (right) was built in 1958. It is a classic example of modern architecture.

Frank Lloyd Wright's "mile-high" skyscraper (left) was never built.

The Hong Kong and Shanghai Bank was completed in 1986.

SIMPLE SHAPE

TRIANGULAR SUPPORTS

REFLECTIVE GLASS CLADDING

Inside out

British architect Norman Foster designed the Hong Kong and Shanghai Bank building in Hong Kong. The building is unusual because its steel frame is on the outside rather than the inside. Double steel columns and triangular supports add to the building's unusual look. Putting the frame on the outside also creates extra space inside the building. New architecture in this distinctive style is sometimes called **post-modernism**.

DOUBLE STEEL COLUMNS

STEEL FRAME ON OUTSIDE

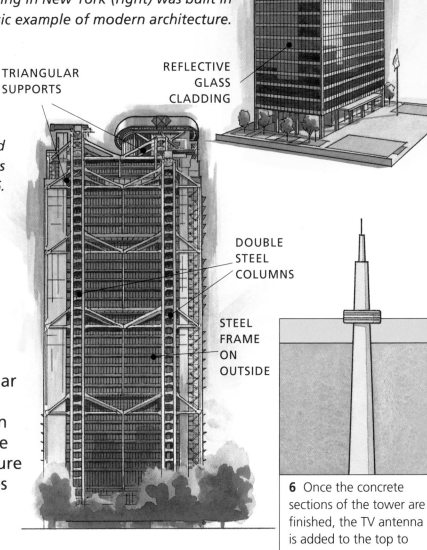

6 Once the concrete sections of the tower are finished, the TV antenna is added to the top to complete the structure.

Skyscraper and Tower Facts

QUICK TIME
The massive Empire State Building in New York City was completed in 1931, after just 18 months work.

TRAGIC DEATHS
Thirty people have committed suicide by jumping from the Empire State Building...

LUCKY ESCAPES
... but two attempts have failed. In 1977, a man jumped from the 86th floor, but landed on a ledge outside the floor below. In 1979, a woman did exactly the same thing.

ON BALANCE
The ironworkers who built the Empire State Building did not wear safety harnesses. Fourteen men were killed in falls and other accidents.

CRASH!
In 1945, a B-25 bomber of the U.S. Air Force flew straight into the 72nd floor of the Empire State Building. It caused extensive damage, but the skyscraper's structure remained sound.

Empire State Building

CN Tower

LIGHTNING NEVER STRIKES TWICE...
But it strikes the top of the CN Tower in Toronto, Canada, an average of 200 times a year.

FOR SALE: EIFFEL TOWER
Government official and super con man Count Victor Lustig sold the Eiffel Tower in Paris for scrap —twice!

Eiffel Tower

BRIGHT LIGHTS
The Marine Tower in Yokohama, Japan is the tallest lighthouse in the world. You can see it 19 miles (32 km) away.

Marine Tower

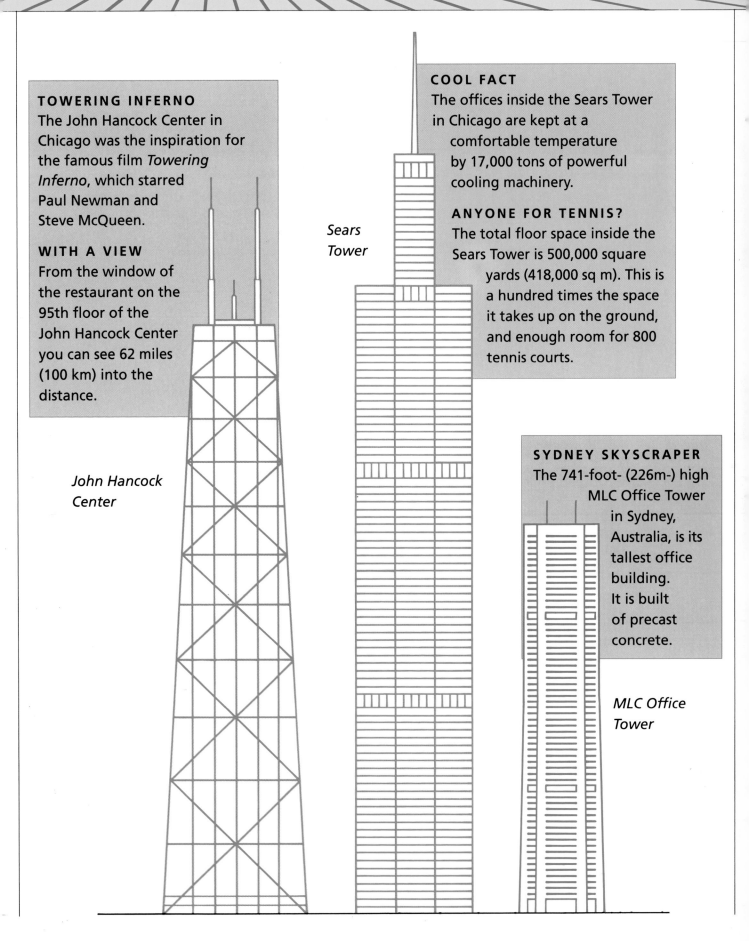

TOWERING INFERNO
The John Hancock Center in Chicago was the inspiration for the famous film *Towering Inferno*, which starred Paul Newman and Steve McQueen.

WITH A VIEW
From the window of the restaurant on the 95th floor of the John Hancock Center you can see 62 miles (100 km) into the distance.

John Hancock Center

Sears Tower

COOL FACT
The offices inside the Sears Tower in Chicago are kept at a comfortable temperature by 17,000 tons of powerful cooling machinery.

ANYONE FOR TENNIS?
The total floor space inside the Sears Tower is 500,000 square yards (418,000 sq m). This is a hundred times the space it takes up on the ground, and enough room for 800 tennis courts.

SYDNEY SKYSCRAPER
The 741-foot- (226m-) high MLC Office Tower in Sydney, Australia, is its tallest office building. It is built of precast concrete.

MLC Office Tower

Time Chart

See how tall buildings have developed into skyscrapers and towers over the centuries. This time chart shows key buildings and when they were built.

> *c stands for circa, or "about." It is used before dates that may not be accurate.*

c 2550 BC
The 480-foot-(146m-) high Great Pyramid of Khufu in Giza, Egypt, commissioned by the pharaoh of the same name, is completed. It remains the world's tallest building for nearly 4,000 years.

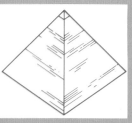

c 270 BC
The 400-foot (122m) Pharos of Alexandria in Egypt, the world's first lighthouse, is built. It is destroyed by an earthquake in the ninth century AD.

1174
The 180-foot-(55m-) high Tower of Pisa, Italy, is begun. It is completed in 1350 and gradually becomes the Leaning Tower of Pisa.

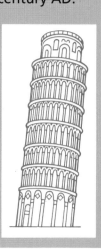

1311
The 525-foot (160m) central tower of Lincoln Cathedral in England is built. Two smaller towers are added in 1420. The central tower falls down in a storm in 1549.

1568
The 502-foot (153m) wood and lead spire of St. Pierre Cathedral in Beauvais, France, is completed.

1854
The American inventor Elisha Otis demonstrates an original model of a safety elevator.

1857
An Otis elevator goes into operation in a five-story china shop in New York City.

1885
The Home Insurance Building, in Chicago, is finished. It is the first modern skyscraper in the world.

1889
The 984-foot (300m) Eiffel Tower in Paris, France, is completed. It remains the world's tallest structure for 40 years.

1890
The spire of Ulm Cathedral in Germany is completed. At 528 feet (161m), it remains the tallest spire in the world.

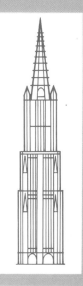

1903
The 285-foot (87m), steel-framed Flatiron Building in New York is completed.

1913
The 795-foot (241m) Woolworth Building in New York City, is completed.

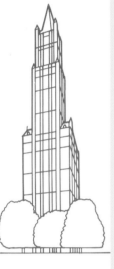

1931
The Empire State Building, New York City, is completed. It remains the world's third tallest occupied building.

1945
A B-25 bomber crashes into the Empire State Building.

1973
The 1,362-foot (415m) World Trade Center, New York City, is completed. It is still the world's second tallest building.

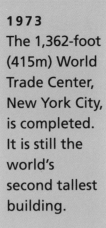

1973
The tallest skyscraper in the world, the Sears Tower in Chicago, is completed. It stands 1,454 feet (443m) above the ground.

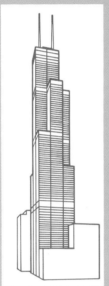

1974
The world's tallest structure, the 2120-foot (646m) Warszawa Radio Mast in Poland, is built. It is supported by guy wires.

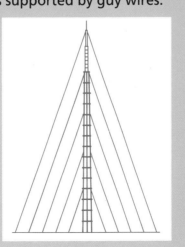

1975
The 1820-foot (555m) CN Tower in Toronto, Canada, is completed. It is the world's tallest unsupported structure.

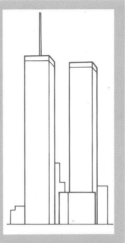

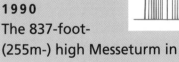

1981
The 886-foot (270m) Statfjord B Oil Platform is completed. It stands in 492 feet (150m) of water.

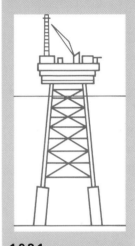

1990
The 837-foot- (255m-) high Messeturm in Frankfurt, Germany, becomes Europe's tallest skyscraper.

1990
At 820 feet (250m), Canary Wharf Tower in London, becomes Britain's tallest skyscraper.

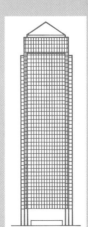

From Start to Finish

On these two pages, you can follow the Step by Step stories in the bottom right-hand corner of each double page from start to finish.

BUILDING A SKYSCRAPER

1 Construction workers must clear away all the old buildings on a site before work on a new skyscraper can begin.

2 A trench is dug around the site and filled with concrete. This retaining wall stops earth movements affecting other buildings.

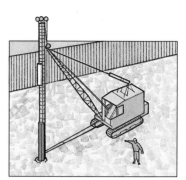

3 A machine called a pile driver pounds metal piles into the ground to make the skyscraper's strong, deep foundations.

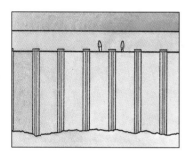

4 The steel piles extend deep into the ground. In some buildings, the base-ment will be built in the space between the piles.

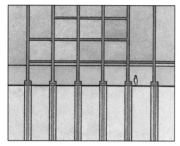

5 After the foundations have been laid, the construction of the steel frame of columns and beams can begin.

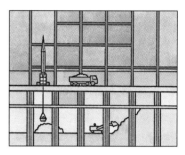

6 As the frame rises, builders begin to construct the basement. This is protected by the retaining wall, which is waterproof.

7 Concrete is poured from a pump over bolted steel sheets, called decking, to make all the floors of the new skyscraper.

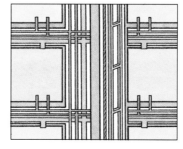

8 Electricity, water supply, and other services are added to the central core of the building as the steel framework grows.

9 Once the frame is nearly complete, builders begin to attach the cladding, the exterior walls, to lower floors.

10 Now the cladding is complete, and the final shape and color of the skyscraper can be seen. But inside, work continues.

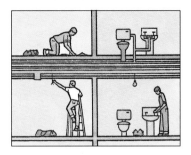

11 Inside the finished skyscraper, subcontractors are working hard to put the finishing touches to services and decor.

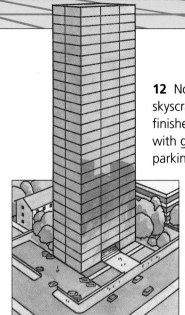

12 Now the skyscraper is finished, complete with gardens and parking areas. The architect's vision has become reality.

BUILDING A TOWER

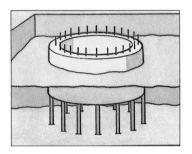

1 First the site for the new tower is cleared. Then strong foundations are built underground to create a firm base.

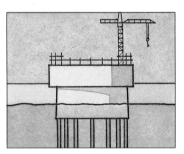

2 Next, a metal slip-forming frame is dropped over the foundations. Concrete is poured into the frame and left to dry.

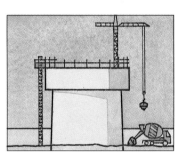

3 The new concrete tower rises slowly from the ground as the massive slipforming machinery moves steadily upwards.

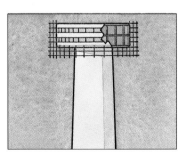

4 When the tower is high enough, an observation platform is built. From here, people will be able to see far into the distance.

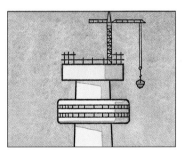

5 Another part of the tower is added using a narrower slipforming frame, as the completed section is fitted out.

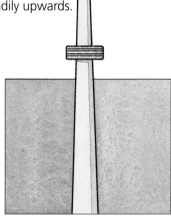

6 Once the concrete sections of the tower are finished, the TV mast is added to the top to complete the structure.

Glossary

architect A person who designs a building inside and out. Architects are often in overall control of a building project.

art deco A style of art which was popular in the 1920s and 1930s. Art deco designs were often based on geometric designs and bold colors.

bolted joint A joint between two or more structural steel sections, made with special high-strength nuts and bolts.

bracing Sections of a building's frame that keep the frame rigid. Bracing does not carry any of the building's weight.

cladding The outer covering of a skyscraper that forms its walls. Cladding hangs on the skyscraper's frame. Also called **curtain wall**.

computer-aided design (CAD) Design that is carried out using a computer. The computer stores all the details of a building and creates drawings based on them.

curtain wall *see* **cladding**

decking Strong interlocking steel sheets over which concrete is poured to make a skyscraper's floors.

framework The strong steel or concrete structure that supports the weight of a skyscraper.

generator A machine that produces electricity from the power of a gasoline or diesel engine.

hoist A temporary lift used to carry materials and workers to the upper floors of a skyscraper under construction.

hopper A large container holding fresh concrete that is lifted by a crane to where it is needed.

hydraulic jack A machine used to lift heavy loads using hydraulic power. To make a jack work, fluid is pumped into a cylinder. The fluid pushes a piston in the cylinder upward.

in situ concrete Concrete that is molded and left to set on a building site rather than in a factory.

ironworkers Construction workers who join together the sections of a skyscraper's steel frame.

laying out The careful measurements carried out before construction of a building starts. Laying out makes sure that the foundations and the framework are built in exactly the right place.

load A force pressing or pulling on a building. The three main loads are **live load** (the weight of the things in a building), **dead load** (the weight of the building itself), and **wind load** (the pressure of the wind on the sides of a building).

main contractor The construction company that is in overall control of a building's construction.

module A section of a building that is self-contained. A whole building can be constructed using combinations of modules.

mold An arrangement of wooden or steel sheets into which concrete is poured. The mold is removed to leave a concrete shape. Also called **formwork**.

pile A steel or concrete column reaching down to solid rock under layers of soft soil. Piles are a type of foundation.

pile driver A machine that hammers steel piles into the ground.

post-modernism A style of architecture popular from the mid-1970s to today, in which each building has its own distinctive look. It often combines elements of many earlier styles.

precast concrete Concrete that is molded and set before it is transported to a construction site.

pressurization system A fire safety system in tall skyscrapers. When a fire starts, air is pumped into corridors and stairwells, making it difficult for smoke to escape from burning rooms.

raft A type of foundation consisting of a large slab of concrete, which "floats" on the ground. A raft is used where piles would be impractical.

reinforced concrete Concrete with steel bars embedded in it. Reinforced concrete is stronger than either concrete or steel.

retaining wall A deep trench filled with concrete that surrounds a construction site. It stops any earth movements caused by construction affecting buildings nearby.

rotary drill A tool like a long screw, used to dig deep holes for concrete piles.

sensors Electronic devices that detect the conditions in a skyscraper, such as temperature and humidity, and feed this information back to a computer control system.

services The systems that supply water, electricity, and fresh air to the floors of a skyscraper, and that take away waste.

slipforming A method of building a concrete structure by continuously pouring concrete into a mold as the mold is moved upward.

structural engineer An engineer who designs the structure of a building, rather than its appearance, and oversees its construction.

stud One of many vertical pieces of wood or metal between a floor and a ceiling that support a lightweight internal wall.

subcontractor A company that carries out specialized jobs that a main contractor cannot do, such as electrical work or plumbing.

supplier A company that provides building materials, such as steel or concrete.

surveyor A person who makes careful measurements of a building site to make sure that everything is in the correct position.

tenement A building with a few floors full of apartments.

tuned-mass damper A device that helps to keep a tall building from swaying too much in strong winds. It is of a massive weight, in the top of the building, whose movements are controlled by a computer.

virtual reality The simulation of a real place using three-dimensional computer graphics. Architects use virtual reality to walk through buildings that only exist in a computer's memory.

welded Joined by adding molten metal between two pieces of metal, or by melting their edges so that they fuse together.

Index

Words in **bold** appear in the glossary on pages 46 and 47.